THE
ATHLETE
IN THE GAME OF LIFE

T0163815

STRETCH, STRENGTHEN, LIVE, AND THRIVE

THE

ATHLETE

IN THE GAME OF LIFE

MATT PEALE NASM CPT, CES

Advantage®

Published by Advantage, Charleston, South Carolina.
Member of Advantage Media Group.

ADVANTAGE is a registered trademark, and the Advantage colophon is a trademark of Advantage Media Group, Inc.

Printed in the United States of America.

10 9 8 7 6 5 4 3 2 1

ISBN: 978-1-64225-237-8
LCCN: 2020919707

Cover design by David Taylor. Layout design by Carly Blake.

This publication is designed to provide accurate and authoritative information in regard to the subject matter covered. It is sold with the understanding that the publisher is not engaged in rendering legal, accounting, or other professional services. If legal advice or other expert assistance is required, the services of a competent professional person should be sought.

Advantage Media Group is proud to be a part of the Tree Neutral® program. Tree Neutral offsets the number of trees consumed in the production and printing of this book by taking proactive steps such as planting trees in direct proportion to the number of trees used to print books. To learn more about Tree Neutral, please visit **www.treeneutral.com**.

Advantage Media Group is a publisher of business, self-improvement, and professional development books and online learning. We help entrepreneurs, business leaders, and professionals share their Stories, Passion, and Knowledge to help others Learn & Grow. Do you have a manuscript or book idea that you would like us to consider for publishing? Please visit **advantagefamily.com** or call **1.866.775.1696**.

This book is dedicated to everyone who wants more out of life and is tired of being in chronic pain. The hardest part is the first step. Congratulations on taking it!

CONTENTS

FOREWORD

I am a middle-aged executive. I know the tightness, aches and pains that naturally come with being fifty-four years old very well. One of my true joys in life is speaking and providing professional development—being in front of groups of people—but the truth is that I spend most of my days in front of a screen. Administering graduate education programs, designing graduate courses, and writing books keep me in front of my computer much more than I care to admit. This naturally comes with its own challenges. Sitting for long periods of time is linked to a number of health concerns including obesity, increased blood pressure, high blood sugar, abnormal cholesterol levels, and weight gain—not to mention the havoc that is wreaked upon muscular and skeletal systems.

Prolonged sitting has also been linked to an increased risk of death from cardiovascular disease and cancer.

The decade of my fifties has also been very hard on me physically. I've had both a laminectomy and microdiscectomy, a fall off my mountain bike that will forever make getting in and out of a car a bit slower, and COVID-19. These setbacks, especially at my age, make it that much more difficult to ensure that I stay physically active every day of my life. But there is the dichotomy. Without question, my body works and feels better when I use it rigorously. Each one of these incidents I've described set me back at least weeks if not months. At my age this can be devastating, but I've conditioned my brain to understand that I need to keep moving. After each one of these setbacks I knew it was worth it to re-engage the physical life. Not only does my body feel better when I use it vigorously, but it performs better as well. I demand a lot of it and it pays me back tenfold. This is also why Matthew Peale's *The Athlete in the Game of Life* is a must read. None of us can escape the aging process but we can make it productive and prosperous through a life of joyful movement.

Matt's book both inspires and teaches. Contained herein are personal anecdotes that we can all identify with and practical ways to combat the physical problems associated with aging and too much sitting. Matt also establishes himself as an expert to provide guidance with these unique issues. What I found to be especially engaging is the way Matt accurately portrays the downside of the executive life. I kept finding myself nodding my head *yes!* as Matt describes executive pain, things like "text neck" or what happens when we sit for too long, in an in-depth and understandable manner. It is extremely important to understand what happens to our bodies and brains as we age, and Matt handles it gracefully even when discussing the issue of fear, which is a critical predictor of decreased physical activity. Most importantly, *The Athlete in the Game of Life* contains many practical applications such as understanding kinetic checkpoints and tips to reduce back pain.

The reason I care so much about remaining an "athlete in the game of life" is because I know firsthand how critical a physical life is to a successful one. There have been junctures in my own history where decisions were made that led to major turning points. Each one of those decisions was preceded by a major physical undertaking. I didn't know it at the time, but I can now connect all the dots. My physical life has always set me up for personal success. The two go hand in hand. My first career as a band director and musician was set up by my venture into competitive bodybuilding. I know that sounds crazy, but I had never played an instrument or read any kind of music until I was almost 21 years of age. Bodybuilding gave me the confidence, drive, desire, and discipline that I had never experienced to that point and allowed me to take the risk of changing majors from business to music. Years later it was the Broad Street Run, a ten-mile road race in Philadelphia, that would lead to the publication of my first book. I didn't win or even finish that high but the act of physically preparing to compete—when I had never run more than four miles in my life—inspired me. When I crossed the finish line, I now knew that I could accomplish anything I set out to do. Eight short months later *The Kinesthetic Classroom: Teaching and Learning through Movement* was published. It was a game changer for me and I can trace it all back to my physical life. Most recently, when my father fell ill and passed away, I was devastated. I wasn't moving, sleeping, or eating the way I should. I knew I needed something to pull me out of this funk and this time I knew what to lean on—my physical life. It was my ability to be on my mountain bike, practice yoga, and weight train that pulled me from depths I had never known. Being physically active had not only changed my life but had also saved it. There is no substitution for a physically active life and as we age the dividends paid for paying attention to it become even greater. It is critical to our health and emotional and intellectual well-being. There's no getting around that. Matthew's book encourages and informs that well-being. Enjoy!

—**Mike Kuczala**, Coauthor, *The Kinesthetic Classroom: Teaching and Learning through Movement*; Coauthor, *Ready, Set, Go! The Kinesthetic Classroom 2.0*; Author, *Training in Motion: How to Use Movement to Create Engaging and Effective Learning*

ACKNOWLEDGEMENTS

All big and important decisions in life start with a seed that grows over time when nurtured. Thank you to No BS Inner Circle / Glazer-Kennedy Insider's Circle at the Orlando SuperConference in 2018 for planting the seed for me to write this book. Along the way many people played a role in watering and fertilizing that seed.

To start, I'd like to thank my parents for various methods of supporting me through the years, and I want to thank my son, Connor, for designing the logo for Compete as an Athlete in the Game of Life as his first graphic design project, at eighteen years old. You have also battled through when I wasn't always the most pleasant person to be around; I love you very much for that. Thank you to my grandparents, aunts, uncles, and cousins, who were there before any of this started; you saw a light in me and helped keep it on.

Fraternity brothers and friends are all family in their own ways, and I couldn't persevere without their help over the years, through many failures and restarts. In no specific order except as you come to mind, I thank you and love you with every fiber of my being: John Reilly, you specifically played a major role in getting this book out—LTH. Kristen Adolfi, Christina Rominger, and the Pearson family—you all stuck by me in Hattiesburg, Mississippi.

And to Gina Tomasella; coworkers, friends, and clients from Franco's Health Club and Spa; the McGuire family; Doug Ellis, my business partner; and my long-term clients who contributed testimonials— from 2015 to this publishing, all of you have been lifesaving and life changing.

Aaron Chow, Jeremy Graves, and Philip La— thank you for your valiant generosity to help my Kickstarter, which unfortunately didn't work. Angel Brookens and Todd Moffatt—thank you for helping to get the funding for this project. Rachel Adams, thank you for helping me get back onto my feet and for promoting this book.

To Tim Hutchings at 24 Hour Fitness in Laguna Hills, California—thank you for hiring me as a personal trainer in the fall of 2008; without your faith, the journey wouldn't have begun. Thank you to all my clients and friends during 2008 to 2011 in south Orange County, California, as I began a new career and followed my passion into fitness. Chris Kavoosi, you know where we come up with the best ideas, sir!

And I thank you, the reader, for having the courage to make a change in your life. Without readers and fans, none of this is possible.

"YOU'RE NOT A KID ANYMORE"

"The first wealth is health."
—RALPH WALDO EMERSON

Howard was thrilled to become vice president. It meant more money, more perks, and more responsibility. This was definitely the move he wanted to make.

So why didn't he feel better?

When he was in his twenties, he felt invincible. He had no aches or pains, and on the rare occasion when something physical did bug him, a couple of Advil tablets did the trick. Now that he was in his forties, it seemed as though he was always hurting. His constant headaches were getting in the way of his ability to concentrate on his work, and every time he went out to play a round of golf, his muscles felt so stiff that his swing was horrible.

Then there was his lower back. It was a mess. Last Tuesday he had to move some heavy boxes to clear out space for his home office but couldn't seem to squat properly to lift them. So he ended up bending over to pick them up ... and that was a *really* big mistake. Now it hurt just to sit.

"You're not a kid anymore, Howie," his wife, Laura, said in the nicest way possible.

No, he wasn't; he had just turned forty-five. But the scary part was that, he thought, *that's not that old.* If he felt this bad at this age, how was he going to feel when he turned fifty? Sixty?

And what the heck could he do about it?

***

There are a lot of men and women who are feeling what Howard's feeling. As they move further into middle age and beyond, they discover their bodies are no longer as resilient as they used to be. When it hurts to get out of bed in the morning, they know there's a problem—especially when things continue to hurt all day long.

There's a reason for that.

Physically, we were not made to live a sedentary lifestyle. When we sit for hours and hours, it puts a different kind of strain on our bodies. Not only that, but staring at so many screens on so many different devices creates other painful outcomes that we'll cover in more detail later. And unfortunately, both sitting and screen-staring are huge components of most people's lives these days.

The COVID-19 pandemic has only worsened this problem. More people are working at home, where they end up being even *less* active, and their life/work balance is completely thrown off. Older adults also can't do all the activities they did before the coronavirus hit—so from all the sitting around, they end up experiencing pain in areas they hadn't before. Naturally, many have turned to medical doctors for relief, but most MDs don't have much to offer, except maybe some stronger pain medication. But that's just like painting over a wall that's cracking apart. Those cracks aren't going away, and sooner or later even the paint isn't going to stop them from reappearing.

Here's the hard, cold truth: if you don't address your pain and stiffness problems now, they're only going to increase in their severity over time. You'll grow less flexible and mobile, which will lead to more of a physical decline than you should have to deal with in your later years. Your bones can weaken. Not only that, but if you don't deal with your body issues now in a proactive way, you could be more likely to experience dementia and Alzheimer's disease when you grow older.

But I'll let you in on a little secret—a good secret: it doesn't have to go that way.

I've always had a passion for health and fitness. After I earned my degree in marketing at the University of Southern Mississippi, I became a National Exercise & Sports Trainers Association personal fitness trainer, and since then I've been certified by the American Council on Exercise, the National Academy of Sports Medicine (NASM), and the National Federation of Professional Trainers. I've worked with clients on weight loss and exercise, taught boot-camp style training, and in 2017 cofounded Movement Academy, where I developed a physical education curriculum and a senior exercise program. My work has been featured in publications; I've spoken at many healthy lifestyle events; and I also hosted "Health and Fitness," an episode of *The Second Half* (on the *Boomers Lifestyle Network*), a show focused on healthy-lifestyle topics for people over the age of fifty-five.

In April 2020 while staying home during the pandemic, I looked for new ways to help my clients.

I found one through becoming a Corrective Exercise Specialist through the NASM, allowing me to bring a whole new level of knowledge and expertise to my clients.

But more importantly, I know how to relate to issues of aging. I'm in my mid-forties, and believe me, if you're in my age range, I feel your pain. Like many, many others, I ended up sitting around too much because of the pandemic. So I quickly looked for answers that would work for me—and my clients.

Fortunately, I already had a lot of knowledge to draw from. A few years ago, I was teaching a senior-fitness circuit class at Franco's Health Club and Spa in Mandeville, Louisiana, where I got more firsthand experience learning about our older population's need for mobility, agility, and balance. Working backward, I could see how they could have entered their golden years in better shape if they had focused on the right things in their middle age. Still, I'm able to help them alleviate their pain points and improve their overall physical well-being.

What I do for people ages forty to eighty is based on the scientific knowledge I've picked up over the years working in this arena. I show them solutions that work—solutions they can't learn from doctors, because, frankly, this isn't subject matter doctors delve into often. And I help them regain the agility and balance of their youth.

Here's what a few of my clients had to say about my coaching:

I would like to let you know how much I have enjoyed and benefited from your training sessions. The exercise and conditioning sessions have improved my balance, strength, and posture. I haven't felt this good in years.

—Don F., certified public accountant

Matt has been my trainer for 4 years. He is extremely knowledgeable about what training I need. He customizes his training sessions, and I have gained strength slowly, without ever feeling hurt physically. He is, as well as all the above, very personable and fun to talk to. I highly recommend him.

—Dr. Karen G., psychologist

I've been working out with Matt twice a week. Since that time, I've seen a significant improvement in my strength and balance, and I have more flexibility in my movements. I have probably doubled the amount of weights

*I can handle. I can now do balance exercises
that were not possible before. I look forward
to continued improvements.*
—Bobbie L., master of science in education

These are typical results for my clients, and I'm
proud to have helped them achieve them. Now I
want to help *you*. For the first time, I'm sharing my
unconventional and proven secrets for how to work
better, play better, and, as a result, *feel* better. You'll
discover how some common, mundane activities in
which we all engage can hit you hard in your pivotal
pain points—*if* you're not aware of how you're using
your body when you do them. And you'll discover a
few simple but highly impactful ways to relieve stress
that your body just wasn't built to endure.

Our friend Howard the VP might not be a kid
anymore, as his wife rightly suggested, but he can definitely *feel* more like a kid if he just takes the advice I'm
about to share in this book—especially if he gets off
his ass and enrolls in one of my programs!

Wishing you health and success,
Matt Peale

CHAPTER ONE

WE ARE ALL ATHLETES

MINDING YOUR BODY THROUGH EVERYDAY LIFE

Before we begin, I want to reassure you of something. Mark Twain once said, "Be careful about reading health books. You may die of a misprint." Well, trust me, this has been well edited: nothing in this book can hurt you!

Now let's talk about you.

Your athletic days may be largely behind you, except for an occasional game of tennis or golf. Maybe you ski once a year; maybe you bike on weekends. Whatever the case, you probably don't think you have to sweat your physical shape that much—it's not as though you have to train for the Olympics or even your high school football team. If you're like most, you just want to keep your weight down and stay relatively healthy.

Staying healthy isn't hard, in your mind, because you don't think you're really doing anything to your body that can hurt you. Maybe you sit and work at your computer most of the day, or you sit with your laptop on your legs and work that way. You probably use your smartphone heavily throughout the day to check on texts and emails, as well as your social media. You know, grown-up stuff.

There's nothing demanding in doing any of that, so there's nothing to worry about, right?

After all, you're not lifting heavy boxes in a warehouse or on a loading dock. You're not doing construction work. How in the world can you hurt yourself sitting on your butt or checking your iPhone?

Well, in fact, you can hurt yourself, and very easily too. No matter what you do, even if it's nothing all that active, it still affects your body in some way— and maybe not in the way you think. I'm about to tell you what can happen; and it's a lot, so you'd better sit down. Scratch that. You'd better stand up!

THE SIDE EFFECTS OF SITTING

Just because you think you're doing nothing doesn't mean your body agrees.

For instance, some part of your body may have started hurting you on a regular basis. It could be your back, your neck, your hips, or another place entirely. And maybe you can't get that part of your body to stop hurting. You ice it, get massages, and try to avoid putting stress on it … yet it's still bugging you constantly, despite the facts that you're not overly active in your day-to-day life and that you're exercising regularly.

First of all, the place that hurts? That pain could be caused by another part of your body entirely. For example, knee pain could be the result of dysfunction or impairment at the hip, ankle, or both. The term for this is *regional interdependence*, a relatively new idea conceived by therapists and rehabilitation professionals as a way to describe how one part of your body depends on the proper functioning of another part.

Second of all, our lives—and our physical health—have been transformed by technology in ways we still don't understand completely. Our work and home environments are filled to the brim with tech gadgets, such as computers, laptops, tablets, smartphones, and even a good old-fashioned TV set or two—and our eyes are glued to the screens of those gadgets for hours every day. Our jobs depend on technology, and our personal lives often revolve around it.

The result? As many as a quarter of all Americans engage in no leisure-time activity at all, according to the US Department of Health and Human Services. This lessens the ability of our bodies' "kinetic chains" to adapt to or to recover from times when we *do* engage in activity, leading to increased injury rates. (We'll get into more detail on the kinetic chain in a later chapter.)

This negative effect on our physicality directly impacts what happens to our bodies twenty years down the road. As I noted, your movements grow less flexible and mobile. When you do play that occasional game of tennis or golf, your motions become stiffer and more limited. A sitting position also puts huge stress onto your back muscles, neck, and spine, especially if you slouch. There's also the issue of postural decline. When you're leaning over to look at your phone or tablet, your body does what's called "remodeling." It adapts to that position and locks it in as your natural state—and that can create some serious pain, because your body simply wasn't built to be in that leaned-over position for long periods of time. For example, you're probably sitting as you read this book, and that caused your body to automatically mold into what you feel is "normal."

We also end up putting on weight. Nobody gains forty pounds in two weeks. You gain that much by putting on a of couple pounds month by month until you wake up and discover you've put on that forty over time. Too much sitting can also raise your risk of heart disease, diabetes, stroke, high blood pressure, and high cholesterol. None of those conditions, obviously, are good things.

Finally, there's one more part of you that can be seriously affected: your mind. At present, sitting and staring at screens can actually boost your anxiety levels. In your future, the damage can get much more serious. According to the National Institutes of Health, a lack of physical activity can boost your chances of Alzheimer's disease, dementia, and cognitive decline.

IF YOU THINK JUST SITTING AROUND MEANS YOU CAN'T GET HURT, WELL, YOU SHOULD PROBABLY THINK AGAIN. CHRONIC PAIN CAN EASILY RESULT FROM THAT LIFESTYLE.

So … if you think just sitting around means you can't get hurt, well, you should probably think again. Chronic pain can easily result from that lifestyle, along with all the other conditions listed above.

THE GOOD NEWS

I've dropped a lot of unpleasant news on you in the preceding section. So now let's look at the bright side. And that bright side is the fact that you can turn things around, thanks to a secret weapon inside your brain that continues to work no matter what your age.

That "weapon" is neuroplasticity, which is the mind's ability to reorganize itself by forming new neural connections throughout your life. Its nerve cells can compensate for aging, injury, and diseases, as well as adjust in response to new situations and changes in lifestyle. For example, when you learn a new language or take lessons to play a new musical instrument, neuroplasticity is what enables you to take on this kind of new and permanent knowledge. But it also allows you to improve your physicality. Even as you grow older, you can still relearn and regain different movements that may have become difficult, or even (you thought) impossible. Neuroplasticity allows you to become incredibly resilient in recapturing your youthful abilities.

In other words, yes, you can reteach an old dog *old* tricks.

When this function of the brain was discovered, most experts believed it was only present in children's brains. It wasn't until late in the last century that experts recognized that neuroplasticity is still at work through the adult years. So even though your brain may have reorganized in a negative way due to your inactive lifestyle, that can be at least partially reversed through the use of an appropriately designed training program. Good physical fitness has been shown to increase the health of your brain's nerve cells (also called *neurons*), which, of course, increases the strength of your neuroplasticity.

Here are a few other benefits that neuroplasticity delivers to us all:[1]

1. Recovery from brain events like strokes

2. Recovery from traumatic brain injuries

3. Enhancement of certain functions to compensate for loss of other functions (for example, a blind person may find their hearing improves due to neuroplasticity)

4. Enhanced memory abilities

5. More effective learning

As I said, physical activity helps increase your neuroplasticity powers. Cardio is an especially effective

1   Courtney E. Ackerman, MSc, "What is Neuroplasticity? A Psychologist Explains," *PositivePsychology.com*, January 9, 2020, https://positivepsychology.com/neuroplasticity/.

kind of exercise that will help you achieve this goal. We'll talk in detail on this topic later on in this book.

RAGING WITH YOUR "MACHINE"

In the next chapter, I'll get into the specifics of how chronic pain can result from sitting too much or constantly leaning over to look at screens, and I'll share some ways to help you find relief.

For the moment, however, I want to remind you that your body is a machine. And all machines need the right fuel to keep them operating at peak efficiency.

If you haven't guessed already, I'm about to talk about a big four-letter word: *diet*.

The first three letters of the word *diet* spell out *die*—and maybe that's why people hate to think about it. But instead, maybe we should all make an effort to stop associating healthy food choices with death! So let's lose the term *dieting* and embrace the good feelings we'll gain just from changing up what we're eating. It can make a big difference to our overall well-being.

Let me break down some primary food categories and how much you should be eating of each.

CARBOHYDRATES

Fruits, vegetables, grains, and beans are all examples of carbs. You'll also find some in nuts and dairy products. Carbs may have been demonized by the media and the no-carb-diet fanatics, but your body likes to use them for energy—so ignore everyone, and put 'em on your plate. You *need* carbs after a workout to replace your glycogen (which helps you maintain your blood-glucose levels). What you want to avoid is processed and sugary goods that contain them.

According to the Institute of Medicine, carbs should make up 45–65 percent of your daily caloric intake.

FATS

Fats are another victim of food prejudice, but in truth, they aren't always bad for you, either. Olive oils, fish, and avocados are all healthy sources of fat, while processed and artificial foods deliver unhealthy fats. In any event, it's almost impossible to eliminate fats from your daily diet entirely, as most foods contain them. Just educate yourself: read food labels, and make sure you're having the suggested serving size to minimize fat consumption. Fats are worse than carbs, because a gram of fat has five more calories than a gram of carbs, so tread carefully.

According to the Institute of Medicine, fats

should make up 20–35 percent of your daily caloric intake.

PROTEINS

As most of you know, meat, eggs, and seafood all contain protein. You'll also find it in beans, legumes, nuts, and dairy. Ingesting protein contributes to a healthy lifestyle, but keto-style diets centering on protein-packed foods isn't recommended for long-term health. To build lean-muscle mass, protein is a must—your muscles use it to rebuild after a workout.

According to the Institute of Medicine, proteins should make up 10–35 percent of your daily caloric intake.

SUPPLEMENTS

Supplements are very popular and can be a part of healthy eating habits. For example, meal replacement shakes can be convenient when you don't have time to eat a normal breakfast, and multivitamins can help you achieve your micronutrient recommendations. I've taken a wide variety of supplements myself to help with sports performance and overall nutrition. I only mention them here because they can fill in the spaces of your dietary objectives.

There's no way around it—your eating habits are critical to your health. You wouldn't put watered-down gas into your car's tank, because its performance would … well, suck. Likewise, you shouldn't put too many unhealthy foods into your body, or you might find yourself feeling run down throughout the day. So try to give your body what it needs, rather than just pounding down awful-for-you snacks like chips, cookies, and crackers all day.

***

Just because you don't live the life of an athlete doesn't mean you shouldn't try to think like one. The truth is, as I've pointed out in this chapter, that you're always using your body, even if you're just standing still or sitting on your butt. So the smart thing to do is to meet its needs and to treat it right. If you do, your body will treat *you* right—and you'll have the strength and agility to "live long and prosper," as *Star Trek*'s Mr. Spock used to say.

However, I will admit that it can be challenging to take care of your physicality when you have an executive lifestyle. In the next chapter, you'll find out why.

CHAPTER TWO
EXECUTIVES

HIGH POSITION, HIGH-LEVEL PAIN?

In the introduction to this book, you met Howard (or "Howie" to his wife, Laura), a high-powered executive who's in a world of hurt in terms of body pain. He may be killing it at his company, but at the same time, he feels like his back pain is killing *him*.

And it's not just his back. It's his neck and his hips ... and then there are those headaches.

"Howie," Laura tells him, "you start work at seven; you're there until at least six at night; and you're sitting 70 percent of the time! You can't keep going on like this. You're moving like an old man, and you're only forty-five!"

Howard understands what she's saying, and he also knows she's right. He just has no idea what to do about it. It's not like he has time to get to the gym to do a two-hour workout every day—or even every other day. But he also knows that his pain is finally starting to affect his job performance. He's getting more irritable; he finds himself unable to concentrate on his work; and he's starting to wake up dreading the day ahead of him because of his aching body.

On weekends he usually manages to get in a game of golf. That used to be his break from the grind. Now it's gradually becoming another ordeal. When he swings his club, he winces with pain, and he can't really swing with the kind of power he used to have. The fun is draining out of the one activity that once relaxed and refreshed him—and as a result he spends more time at "the nineteenth hole" rather than the other eighteen.

Howard doesn't understand what's happening to him; he just knows he needs help. If he can find a way to feel better, he'll enjoy his life again.

But how?

UNDERSTANDING EXECUTIVE PAIN

Howard's plight is typical of the troubles afflicting many executives. Years of hunching over and staring at a device or computer screen can pull your body in directions contrary to its design. As noted in the last chapter, your body ends up remodeling, which then causes discomfort and back pain when you stand up straight. Sometimes the simplest physical tasks, such as squatting to pick something up or reaching to take something off a high shelf, can suddenly become increasingly difficult.

And even though you, like Howard, may engage in activities like tennis and golf or even regular exercise, the pain just won't go away.

What's causing this? Well, when the body remodels, it can create muscle imbalances, which, if not corrected, cause ongoing aches and pains. A muscle imbalance is when certain muscles in the body are stronger or more developed than other corresponding muscles, so they no longer work together like they should—one muscle ends up contracting and tightening up, because the corresponding muscle is too weak to counteract that force and pull it back all the way. That weaker muscle becomes elongated as a result.

This can create a multitude of physical issues, such as pain and limited mobility. Muscle imbalances can also lead to an increased risk of injury because your overall balance is affected by a lack of stability. This instability, in turn, can lead to an increased risk of damage to joints, muscles, bones, tendons, ligaments, and the surrounding connective tissue.

Here are some typical symptoms of muscle imbalances:

- Propensity for low back injuries, due to the body's inability to activate muscles around the hips while a person picks up objects or engages in physical activity

- Tension headaches and a lack of rotation for golf and tennis swings, caused by hunched-over shoulders and a forward-leaning head

- Higher chance of ACL injuries from lateral lower body movements, due to inwardly rotated knees

- Achilles-tendon damage and ankle problems, due to calf-muscle inflexibility caused by high-heeled shoes

Now let's dig deeper into two of the biggest physical problem areas for executives: the neck and hip muscles. We'll start with the neck and work our way down.

"TEXT NECK"

"Text neck" is a term coined by Dr. Dean Fishman, after he noticed more and more people were coming to his office with the same complaint: they all had neck pain, headaches, shoulder pain, or numbness and tingling in the upper extremities. This was concurrent with the rapid rise of smartphone usage.

In studies of the new phenomenon, it was found that text neck (also called "iHunch" by some) leads to premature wear-and-tear on the spine and degeneration. It has also become a pretty widespread condition.

"It is an epidemic or, at least, it's very common," Dr. Kenneth Hansraj, chief of spine surgery at NY Spine & Rehab Medicine, told the *Washington Post*. "Just look around you, everyone has their heads down."[2]

You may ask, "So what's the big deal with putting your head down to check out an email?"

Fair enough. Let's start with the fact that the typical human head weighs about twelve pounds. And the neck is fine with holding that amount of weight

---

2   Lindsey Bever, "'Text Neck' Is Becoming an Epidemic and Could Wreck Your Spine," *Washington Post*, November 20, 2014, https://www.washingtonpost.com/news/morning-mix/wp/2014/11/20/text-neck-is-becoming-an-epidemic-and-could-wreck-your-spine/.

up; it was made to carry heads around, right?

Right. However …

When you bend that neck forward and down to check out something on your phone, the weight impact increases on your cervical spine (the structure of bones, nerves, muscles, ligaments, and tendons that extends from the base of your skull to the top of your shoulders). For example, at a fifteen-degree angle, your head puts twenty-seven pounds of pressure onto your neck. At a thirty-degree angle, it's forty pounds. At sixty degrees, it's sixty pounds.

> AT A FIFTEEN-DEGREE ANGLE, YOUR HEAD PUTS TWENTY-SEVEN POUNDS OF PRESSURE ONTO YOUR NECK. AT A THIRTY-DEGREE ANGLE, IT'S FORTY POUNDS. AT SIXTY DEGREES, IT'S SIXTY POUNDS. THAT'S A LOT.

That's a lot.

Imagine carrying an eight-year-old around your neck several hours a day (and just imagine it; don't try to actually do it!), and you'll get the idea.

As you stretch the tissue for a long period of time, it gets sore and inflamed. That causes muscle strain, pinched nerves, and herniated disks; over time, it can even remove the neck's natural curve. The other thing to keep in mind is that you're also engaging in poor posture when you're in the text-neck position, and that causes other problems. Experts say it can reduce lung capacity by as much as 30 percent, as well as cause neurological issues, depression, and heart disease.

Oh, and those headaches you might think are being caused by the tension and stress of your job? The truth is that they're likely being caused by text neck. Headaches, a common symptom of text neck, feel exactly like tension headaches … but aren't.

I know it seems silly to think that all these bad things can happen just as a result of staring at your smartphone. But google "text neck," and you'll see for yourself—these physical outcomes are all the real deal.

ON YOUR BUTT AND IN PAIN

I have a client who has no choice—she has to sit on the job.

That's because she's an amputee, who lost her left lower leg in a lawn-mower accident as a child. She now works in medicine, assisting surgeries for most of the day and working in her office for the remaining hours—and during all that time, she's sitting. When she started experiencing pain because of it, she came to me. Since I'm a Corrective Exercise

Specialist (CES), I was able to assess the pain and work with her in addressing the dysfunction in her hips and hamstrings, the result of prolonged sitting.

Many fitness trainers, however, ignore those particular muscles. They're used to guys who want to bulk up the upper half of their bodies and women who focus on glutes, quadriceps, triceps, and anything abdominal related. So I felt gratified and validated when my client showed me an article in a magazine dedicated to helping amputees in all aspects of life. The article suggested all the exercises I had instructed her to do in previous sessions to increase mobility and strength in her hamstrings and hips—and she was impressed that I knew to focus on those muscles, since I had never worked with an amputee before. I told her it was simply a result of all my experience working with executives and other individuals who were relatively sedentary—I had learned over time where the physical problems hit the hardest and how to correct those imbalances.

It all centers on the hips. From an evolutionary standpoint, we weren't built to sit for long periods of time. Your muscles have to work overtime to support that position, and you end up stretching your hamstring muscles, tightening your quadriceps, and remodeling your hips. Also, nerves can become compressed, and common issues such as sciatica (back pain) can occur.

When you stop sitting and decide to get upright, you've got more potential problems on your hands—or more accurately, in your hips. When you go to stand up, you end up trying to put the pelvis back into a standing position, and some of these muscles get irritated and strained in the process. Lower-back pain is a frequent result. The hips, while often overlooked, are critical to the alignment of your legs and torso. They must be strong to do that job; but sitting weakens them, and gravity suddenly becomes your worst enemy. Your legs will collapse inward, put pressure onto your kneecaps, and eventually cause flat feet.

But at any rate, now you're standing. When you go ahead and take a step, however, since the hips are no longer strong enough to hold themselves up, you end up with hip pain. Meanwhile, the lower back tries to take some of the burden off the hips—and that's not good for the lower back. The pain that results travels up the spine and into your neck. You can also end up throwing out your lower back.

All of this negatively affects your posture, because you're twisting your muscles into positions they don't much care for. Those muscles become strained, creating more weakness in your body.

The fact is that mobility in the hips is key to movement in all directions. The glutes are the largest muscle of the body and are responsible for producing power when you squat, lunge, jump, swing a golf club, pick up a bag of mulch, and perform all other movements related to bending at the knee and lowering your hips. All those movements become much more difficult when your hips lack the strength and flexibility to function properly. As you grow older, you begin to have basic balance issues, and falls are the unfortunate result. I actually see this developing in people as young as their early forties!

***

The physical perils of the executive lifestyle are usually ignored. Most focus on the mental toll that a high-pressure position can take—and they blame that stress even for their most severe aches and pains.

Believing there's nothing they can do to find relief, too many executives grit their teeth and bear the pain like Howard does. Or they seek solutions that don't solve the complete problem. Orthopedic surgeons want to operate on you; a chiropractor limits their work to just your spinal column area; and due to health insurance rules, a physical therapist can only address a specific injury. Unfortunately, none of these professionals will attack the real problem, because that's not where their expertise lies. But that's how I help my clients every day.

Believe me, as time goes on, these physical challenges do not go away. If anything, they grow more difficult to navigate. Tune in to the next chapter to learn more about tackling those challenges.

CHAPTER THREE

AGING AND ACTIVE

KEEPING YOUR HEALTH YOUNG AT HEART

L et's take our friend Howard into the future. Let's say he's been retired for a few years and has just celebrated his seventieth birthday.

One day in the kitchen, he finds himself falling for almost no reason—his balance is just off. He's been noticing that happening a lot, but this is the first time it put him on the floor. Now he's shaken up and freaked out. He had just read some research online that if you fall once, you're very likely to fall again, and he didn't want to be a part of that statistic.

That same day, he happens to look closely at himself in the mirror and notices ...

What the &%$#? I'm shrinking?

He looks smaller than he used to, and he doesn't

get why. Is this his imagination? … Nope. He checks his height, and he's two inches shorter than he was!

Howard was enjoying his retirement, but now his body seems to be fighting him every step of the way. He has constant back pain and shuffles more than he walks. Since the fall, his confidence in his ability to move around has plummeted—he holds on to whatever's nearby to keep himself steady, whether he needs the support or not. And while he's still playing golf twice a week with some old work buddies, his swing is dramatically shorter than just a few years ago, and most of his distance is gone.

Then one day Laura sees him putting on his shoes and notices they were already tied. When she asks him about it, he answers (with more than a little embarrassment) that he never unties them anymore. He puts them on and takes them off with the laces already in place, because it's just too painful for him either to bend down or to bring each foot up to deal with them. More alarmingly, Laura has noticed that sometimes Howard will repeat sentences or completely forget what they had been talking about.

Laura insists on him going to the doctor, but all the tests show nothing's wrong. Yet something clearly is. She's starting to wonder if he'll make it to seventy-five—and if he does, will he need a caregiver to help him? Will they need to move into assisted living?

Howard may not be sitting at a desk eight to ten hours a day, but he still hasn't grappled with the physical effects of aging. He thinks there's nothing he can do about it. The years go by, and you fall apart, right? What are you gonna do? Doctors only treat you when you're sick, and Howard's not sick; he's just old.

Well, what Howard doesn't know is that there are specific things you *can* do to stay active and healthy. I help my clients learn these techniques every day, and they let me know what a huge difference these techniques make to their everyday lives.

In reality, there is nothing substantially wrong with Howard except for the fact that he's getting older. So let's dig deeper into what happens to our bodies once we reach our golden years, and let's learn what we can do about it.

THE EFFECTS OF AGING

As much as you might want to pretend aging isn't going to slow you down, the truth is that it will—if you don't take steps to mitigate its effects. There are a lot of things that can go wrong if you're not careful, and they can definitely impact your quality of life. For instance:

BONES, MUSCLES, AND JOINTS

Howard wasn't having a hallucination when he looked in the mirror and noticed he seemed physically smaller. Bones shrink over time (and also lose density, which makes fractures more likely). You lose muscle mass, which can also make you appear smaller. Your tendons and joints become stiffer and make you less mobile—and create the balance issues Howard is experiencing. And just like Howard, you can even lose an inch or two from your height, from the shrinkage of your spine.

All of these physical changes can reduce your range of motion, which takes its toll on everything from playing a simple game of golf or tennis to getting dressed in the morning.

THE CARDIOVASCULAR SYSTEM

Over time, most people experience a stiffening of the blood vessels and arteries, causing the heart to work harder so that it can pump blood through them. Although the heart muscles will adjust to this increased strain, the risk of high blood pressure will increase.

YOUR MIND

Your brain also changes as the years roll by, and that might have a minor effect on memory and thinking skills. Even a healthy older adult might forget a familiar name or have more difficulty multitasking. There is also, unfortunately, the possible development of dementia, in which memory problems become more severe.

FEAR

OK, I bet you didn't expect to see that four-letter word sitting there. Fear isn't something that instantly comes to mind when you think about aging, but it's a bigger problem than you might imagine. And one specific fear can really cause chaos: the fear of falling.

Here's a startling fact: older adults fear falling more than robbery, bankruptcy, or health problems.

This fear is a better predictor of decreased physical activity than age, health, gender, prescription-medication use, or history of previous falls. Less physical activity, however, causes fear-afflicted seniors *more* disability, not less. They begin to do fewer normal daily activities such as bathing and shopping. They often slow their speed, widen their stance, and make other adjustments that badly affect their balance.

And weirdly enough, that fear of falling *increases* the possibility of falls, which in turn increases the risk of having to enter a healthcare facility and even losing their independence.

According to the Centers for Disease Control

and Prevention (CDC), falls are the leading cause of trips to the emergency room for older adults and seniors, as well as the leading cause of fatal injury. It's difficult to gauge how many of those falls are the result of fear, but you can bet it's a big percentage.

But you don't have to be afraid when you cross the sixty-five-year line. You can remain confident in your physical abilities a lot longer—and that will cause you to enjoy your golden years a whole lot more.

The best way to stay as ageless as possible is through proper diet and exercise. Physical activity is especially important because it increases your blood flow and keeps you limber. It even improves brain function and reduces stress and depression, which can harm your memory.

And there's one more secret weapon I mentioned briefly earlier in this book: neuroplasticity.

HOW NEUROPLASTICITY KEEPS YOU AGELESS

I've just dropped a lot of bad news onto you about aging. Now let's talk about the good news.

A CES like me can help you delay and possibly prevent these symptoms of nature with an exercise prescription that has no negative side effects. The only thing you might suffer is addiction—an addiction to feeling good, having more energy, and having a clearer mind.

Luckily for us, the human body is a wonderful machine that—if treated properly—can regenerate strength, coordination, and balance and can build brain cells through the wonder of neuroplasticity. Even though I'm in my mid-forties, I've proven this for myself. Using exercises specifically designed to activate neuroplasticity, I have prevented my coordination and balance from declining like they do with others my age. I have better mobility and range of motion, which improve my golf swing. My posture has also improved, because I'm aware that I must focus more on standing up straight.

> LUCKILY FOR US, THE HUMAN BODY IS A WONDERFUL MACHINE THAT—IF TREATED PROPERLY—CAN REGENERATE STRENGTH, COORDINATION, AND BALANCE AND CAN BUILD BRAIN CELLS THROUGH THE WONDER OF NEUROPLASTICITY.

That awareness is key. You might not notice that you kind of slump over or that your shoulders are rounded. A lot of my clients don't see it for themselves until I point it out. However, when you are aware and when you do make an effort to improve, you create a healthier "new normal" for your body, which remodels itself to a posture that's more natural and that gives you a better physical appearance. Because I've incorporated what I teach into my life, I've noticed the difference for myself.

Again, this is possible because our brains possess the power of neuroplasticity, which we all can access even when we get older. Here are the basics:

- Neuroplasticity is the brain's ability to reorganize itself throughout life by forming new neural connections.

- Neuroplasticity allows the neurons in the brain to compensate for aging, injury, and disease and to adjust their activities in response to new situations or to changes in their environment.

- Neuroplasticity makes your brain extremely resilient and is the process by which all permanent learning takes place. You're only able to learn how to speak a new language or how to play a different musical instrument because of neuroplasticity.

In other words, it's never too late to get your body closer into the shape it was when you were younger.

Yes, years of sitting may have remodeled your body, causing you aches and pains that never seem to go away. But because the brain retains a lifelong capacity for plasticity and adaptive reorganization, that negative remodeling can be at least partially reversed through the use of an appropriately designed training program.

Studies have also shown that the brain itself benefits from neuroplasticity. Improvements in memory functions occur from cardiovascular exercise, even something as simple as going for a walk. Low-intensity workouts involving coordination and resistance exercise also improve cognition skills, regardless of age, according to recent studies.

What's most beneficial in terms of accessing your neuroplasticity is a comprehensive exercise program. That program should include cardiovascular exercise, balance and stability exercises, resistance training, and coordination training. It's also important to exercise your mind as well as your body, because it can be a matter of "use it or lose it." Many older adults park themselves in front of the TV and don't challenge their brains. That's why cognitive exercises are important—and they can be a lot of fun at the same time. Here are a few that professionals recommend:

- Meditation

- Thought-provoking conversations

- Classes in subjects such as art and language

- Nature walks with others

- Jigsaw puzzles

- Crossword and Sudoku puzzles

- Word games and logic puzzles

All of these types of activities stimulate your mind in different ways and keep you from experiencing "brain drain."

The bottom line for older adults and those in their second phase of life is that there is *no* age at which a strong mental and physical exercise program can't reward you by allowing you to establish and to maintain a healthy and active lifestyle.

However, this kind of program isn't going to come from a doctor. Even if they are aware of neuroplasticity, they probably don't know how best to leverage this innate ability. What really benefits your brain power is elevating your heart rate to at least 60 percent of its maximum. That's how you harness the power of BDNF 1 (brain-derived neurotrophic factor 1), which is the only way you can build brain cells in the hippocampus portion of your mind. Cognitive exercises alone won't do it.

My training has allowed me to help my clients, including older adults, improve their lives, based on the science of neuroplasticity. I eliminate the "how, what, and why" for them and give them each a personalized prescriptive exercise program that can be done at home or at a gym. I also give them the option to include customized coaching and nutritional guidance. My goal is always to help them stretch, strengthen, live, and thrive, so that no matter what age they are, they can get back into the game of life and play it better than ever.

In the next chapter, I'm going to delve into a subject that applies to adults of all ages—the body's most problematic pain points and how to address them. So put down the Advil, and give this a read—it might just provide the relief you're looking for!

CHAPTER FOUR
PRIME PAIN AREAS

THE FIVE KINETIC CHECKPOINTS
YOU NEED TO KNOW ABOUT

When we move less, we end up hurting more. It's as simple as that.

As I've noted throughout this book, computers and mobile devices have completely changed our lifestyles. We constantly feel the need to look at the electronic screens that surround us. That causes us to contort our bodies into positions that are unnatural, so our bodies feel the need to adapt. After all, they're just doing what we tell them to do … you can't blame them for trying!

The trick is to work *with* your body, not against it.

According to the CDC, as many as a quarter of all Americans engage in no leisure-time activity at all.[3] Obviously, the pandemic has worsened this phenomenon. The same agency has determined that lack of regular physical activity creates a kinetic chain in your body that is no longer prepared for movement when you *do* engage in activity. That leads to more pain and more injuries because your body just can't function like it should—it has "unlearned" how it should respond to normal physical movement.

Think of your body—when you're in good shape—as a well-oiled machine. Like a machine, it's made up of otherwise-fixed parts that joints mobilize. A "kinetic chain" simply means that all these joints and parts influence each other when they move. When you don't spend as much time moving as you should, those effects are negative, because everything is … well, out of whack. Disruption at just one link can alter the functioning of the entire chain. When you practice good posture, your parts interact as they should. When you constantly slump or sit or tilt your neck forward to look at a smartphone, they don't. That's why the best exercises to do as you get older are ones that address proper kinetic-chain function, so that you can reduce or hopefully even eliminate pain

---

3   "Physical Activity and Health," Centers for Disease Control and Prevention, last updated November 17, 1999, https://www.cdc.gov/nccdphp/sgr/concl5.htm.

when you do something physical.

Here's a simpler way to visualize this: think of the kinetic chain as your least favorite freeway—you know, one where the traffic is consistently heavy. Normally traffic moves OK because there are enough lanes to prevent much backup. *But* … if there's an accident at, say, Exit 3, and you're trying to get onto the freeway at Exit 1, you may discover that the traffic's too backed up for you to get on easily—and once you do manage to get on, you end up not moving for an hour.

But the problem isn't really at Exit 1—it's the Exit 3 collision that screwed things up. In other words, that entire stretch of road is disrupted because of one trouble spot caused by that accident. Well, when one "link" in your kinetic chain isn't working right, it can mess up another link. That means pain can occur at one point, but that pain is caused by *another* point. For example, pain in your knees can be caused by dysfunction in your ankles when you jog or run.

THE FIVE KINETIC CHECKPOINTS

There are five primary "checkpoints" in your body's kinetic chain. At any of these five checkpoints, chronic pain can develop if you're not using your body as you should. Not only that, but also, as I said, the pain in one checkpoint may be caused by strain on *another* checkpoint, because all five rely on each other to function properly.

Let's go through each of the five individual checkpoints, so that you can see what I'm talking about.

CHECKPOINT #1: FEET AND ANKLES

Your feet and ankles are the first body parts to feel the impact of walking or running. The more flexible they are, the better your body can handle that impact.

> SOMEONE EXPERIENCING PAIN IN THE BACK AND HIPS MIGHT NEVER EVEN CONSIDER THAT IT COULD BE CAUSED BY A LACK OF ANKLE MOBILITY. IN AN EARTHQUAKE, THE UPPER FLOORS OF A BUILDING CAN BE DAMAGED IF THE GROUND FLOOR ISN'T STABLE.

But when these parts lack mobility, it can impact another checkpoint. Someone experiencing pain in the back and hips might never even consider that it could be caused by a lack of ankle mobility. In an earthquake, the upper floors of a building can be damaged if the ground floor isn't stable. Well, the same effect can happen in your body.

High heels and other dress shoes with elevated

heels are another big offender that limits flexibility at this checkpoint, for women and men alike. These shoes can cause tightness in calf muscles, which in turn forces the knees and hips to compensate by using other muscles for stabilization and movement. If you have a problem bending over to tie your shoes or to pick up a box, the culprit could be your ankles.

CHECKPOINT #2: KNEES

Your knees rely on the proper functioning of the joints above and below them. Again, pain in this region may not result from a lack of mobility specifically in the knee; it may be coming from tightness in the ankles or hips.

When you sit for long periods of time, the quadriceps on top of your thighs can become tight, which can cause pain in the hips and knees. If you do work out and try to incorporate lunges, squats, or deadlifts into your routine, you may find you can't fully bend your knees, because of a lack of flexibility in the ankles and hips. If this is the case, you may notice your knees moving together during a squat-type movement.

CHECKPOINT #3: LPHC

Shakira famously sang, "My hips don't lie," and that is an absolutely true statement. If they're having a problem, they'll be honest with you and hurt like hell!

LPHC is short for lumbopelvic-hip complex, which encompasses your lower back and hips. This complex is in an extremely important position, because it's the connection point between your upper and lower bodies. Sitting too much creates many spinal and muscle dysfunctions in this area, which affect your overall posture. The most common imbalances that result from sitting and leaning toward a screen are a shift downward in the hips and an overextension of the upper back and neck.

If you have a desk job and commute to work, you're sitting a *lot*. Think about it. You're sitting in your car to go sit at your desk, and that time will only be broken up by you going somewhere and sitting to eat lunch. Worse, you may go home and sit and watch TV after all that. Yes, it's a sit-a-thon, and this kind of lifestyle is the top cause of back and neck pain. Even if you're an avid gymgoer, not addressing these specific issues can worsen these problems and make you more prone to injury. And if you're a golfer or tennis player, you might find your body can't rotate to generate the power needed for a swing in either sport.

CHECKPOINT #4: SHOULDERS AND THORACIC SPINE

This is the area where you may experience a decreased range of motion, which, as I mentioned, can interfere with your daily life, as well as activities such as golf and tennis. You might have pain with movements in certain directions or be unable to move your shoulders due to a pinch or block. It can also be difficult to put your hand behind your back to reach, say, a back pants pocket or the clasp of a bra.

Your shoulder is a fairly complicated joint, with your shoulder blade "floating" above the ribs and your thoracic spine serving as the foundation. When you slouch, the entire shoulder complex can be driven forward, which places stress on the joint and limits your range of motion. In other words, poor posture is what drives negative effects in this area.

CHECKPOINT #5: CERVICAL SPINE AND HEAD

This is where "text neck," which we talked about previously, comes into play. Almost everyone in today's world has this condition to some extent, because everyone's always looking down at their phones! You can spot text neck when you see rounded shoulders and a forward-tilted head.

This might not seem like a big deal, but here's why you should pay attention to it. As you age, the body naturally curves from loss of fluid in spinal discs. A condition like text neck speeds up this natural decline and can make you appear older than you are. And again, this affects other parts of your body, which literally close off from being hunched over. The result? Tension headaches. Yes, chiropractors can work on misalignments in the spine and bring you temporary relief, but if you don't stretch and strengthen the correct muscles, those headaches will be back (and you'll be back to the chiropractor) in no time.

Then there's the pain that can develop in the neck itself. According to the Mayo Clinic, neck pain is the fourth leading cause of disability, and over a third of the population will suffer from it. The study also showed that women are much more likely to experience this health problem than men; and, if an individual is under severe stress, the risk of neck pain increases by one and a half times.[4]

***

---

4   Stephen P. Cohen, MD, "Epidemiology, Diagnosis, and Treatment of Neck Pain," *Mayo Clinic Proceedings* 90, no. 2, (February 2015): 284–99.

So those are the five body checkpoints you have to watch as you get older, especially if you have a mostly sedentary lifestyle. In the next chapter, I'll give you some helpful tips on getting your kinetic chain back on track, so that all your parts work in unison as they should!

CHAPTER FIVE
THE "EXERCISE PRESCRIPTION"

HOW TO STRETCH AND STRENGTHEN FOR YOUR DAILY DOINGS

O K, so you have bad posture from sitting and tilting your head forward to look at screens. How do you fix it?

Well, you can change your job or your daily sitting habits. But that's not very realistic, is it? Your other option is to work with a CES such as myself, someone specifically trained to work with these areas.

The usual personal trainer just isn't enough. They are out to get you into shape, and there's nothing wrong with that. But they aren't educated in tackling the specific pain issues encountered by those forty and older, due to their lifestyles. A CES is. When your body has undergone years of mistreatment, it requires a specialist like a CES to help you get back into the game of life at the level you want to reach.

The first thing a CES will do is analyze your physical problems through a scientific series of assessments. The CES will then help you by giving you exercises that will bring everything into harmony over a nine-month period if done properly. Each joint area is stretched and strengthened in a systematic method to ensure your areas of pain and tightness are resolved. Again, a chiropractor will only bring you temporary relief, and an MD probably won't know what to tell you; they'll just prescribe some pain pills. But unlike other specialists, a CES has the specific training to help you fix your pain and restore your mobility in a healthy and organic way, with an exercise prescription that's specific to your needs.

THREE SECRET TIPS TO REDUCE BACK PAIN

Let me share three ways a CES will help you alleviate back pain. Again, you won't get these tips from a doctor or personal trainer. In fact, other trainers come to me for help in diagnosing their clients' issues. They know that if you want the best care, you have to work with the best. And these are issues that can be crucial to your day-to-day life. Complications relating to back and neck pain are leading causes of missed work and workers' compensation claims. One misstep with a bad back, and you could miss weeks of work or even cause permanent damage, depending on your age.

I've found that most people just don't know how to exercise to fix these kinds of problems. Most will stand up, bend over, and touch their toes to stretch out their backs. This might feel good in the moment, but

THIS MIGHT FEEL GOOD IN THE MOMENT, BUT IN TRUTH, YOU'RE DOING MORE HARM THAN GOOD AND ARE ACTUALLY PULLING YOUR BODY MORE OUT OF BALANCE.

in truth, you're doing more harm than good and are actually pulling your body more out of balance.

People who are sedentary or sit for long periods of time typically have subtle changes in their body's alignment. The hips shift downward, pulling the lower back out of alignment. The upper back and shoulders round forward from leaning over to look at a screen. Additionally, the head tilts forward (text neck), pulling the neck out of alignment, which can cause headaches and give them the appearance of being shorter. Even if they work out regularly, chances are that they're not doing much stretching to begin with … and their posture will suffer even more when they lift weights.

Here are three things they—and you—can do about it.

SECRET #1: STRETCH THE HIP FLEXORS, NOT THE HAMSTRINGS

When you stretch by touching your toes, you're lengthening a muscle that is already stretched beyond its normal length. When your hips tip downward on your front side, the backside hamstrings are pulled into a lengthened position. Sitting already causes your hamstrings to stretch naturally, but when you add up the hours, days, months, and years of this kind of stretching, your lower back gets pulled out of alignment and causes you pain.

So don't touch your toes. Instead, use leg curls and glute bridges to strengthen the hamstrings and glutes, and stretch your hip flexors and quadriceps (the top of your thighs) with forward lunge stretches while keeping the back leg straight—or stand on one leg and grab the ankle of your other leg, pulling your foot toward your glutes.

SECRET #2: OPEN YOURSELF UP

When you see an older person shuffling down the street, bent over and looking like a shell of their former self, you may feel lucky you don't look like that. However, in reality, you could be well on your way to the same physical shape. Between typing away on your computer and your phone and using the steering wheel of your car, your shoulders and upper back will round off and make you resemble the Hunchback of Notre-Dame!

Your thoracic spine has a natural twenty- to forty-degree curvature. Years of leaning and bending at this junction can give you the appearance of losing your height. To counteract this trend, stretch your chest and abdominals, while strengthening your middle and upper back muscles. Here's how: To stretch your chest, stand in a doorway with your arm in an *L* position, then lean forward while keeping good posture. To strengthen those back muscles, bend over backwards with dumbbells or a barbell.

Stop doing all the crunches—unless you really like that rolled-into-a-ball look. (In that case, keep going!)

SECRET #3: FLATTEN THE CURVE

Flattening the curve might be more necessary for women than men. Wearing high heels all day, especially while sitting, contributes even more to overlengthened hamstrings and glutes, while the calf muscles can become extremely tight in their elevated positions. Combine these physical factors, and you wind up with reduced flexibility in the ankles, hips, and low back.

To combat these issues and to reduce pain, stretch your calf muscles while strengthening your shins, hamstrings, and glutes. Do a standing calf stretch: with just your toes, stand on a step, and let your heels drop naturally to stretch your calf muscles. For hamstrings, stand on one leg, hinge at the hip and reach down to touch your foot. Repeat for both legs, performing one to two sets of twelve reps. For your shins, walk like you're wearing swim fins: point your toes up as high as you can with your heels on the ground for each step. Walk twenty steps like this.

Guys, you might not be totally off the hook. Depending on the size heel in your dress shoes, you might also experience similar pains and not realize why. If you're a tennis or racquetball player, tight calf muscles can lead to torn Achilles tendons and possibly a torn ACL (anterior cruciate ligament).

Those injuries, on top of low back pain, make for a miserable time, so the same advice goes for you—stretch those calf muscles, and strengthen your shins, hamstrings, and glutes.

***

These are only general steps toward resolving the kinds of physical problems I've talked about in this short book, because you really need a personal assessment in order to get specifics that will work for you. Everybody has different issues that need different answers, so I hope you seek out a CES who can provide those answers. That CES can be me, as I do work with my clients virtually.

Find out how you can be part of my team (and take advantage of a great offer) next!

CONCLUSION

I've got a question for you: Want to be part of my Athlete in the Game of Life team? I will tell you that it's not for everyone. But if you …

- Want more out of your active hobbies and interests but feel limited by chronic pain

- Have hit a plateau in your fitness or active interests, due to long hours of inactivity in your career or stage of life

- Want to be challenged, to be held accountable, and to learn new ways to enhance your healthy, active lifestyle

… then you're an excellent candidate. And as a team member, you will receive:

- Monthly webinars on upping your game for the physical activities you enjoy most

- Opportunities to participate in healthy-and-active-lifestyle travel retreats

- Discounts on nutritional products and live online and in-person events

- Monthly newsletters with tips on golf, tennis, hiking, gardening, and other activities

- An online private discussion group to share your ideas and experiences with others

You can also get a free copy of this book—if you're reading someone else's at the moment—and whatever books I will be writing in the future!

Best of all, being a part of my Athlete in the Game of Life Team only costs you $19.97 a month, and you can cancel at any time if you don't find value in my program. (Now, personally, I think you will, but I'm saying that to keep the lawyers happy.) I think it's a small price to pay to get your game back in every area of your life.

Here are a couple more reviews from satisfied clients, and then I'll tell you how to join up:

I just have to say, Matt you are the best and many thanks for helping me! After I really injured my back badly (which turned out to be my hip) and after months of rehabilitation, you took the time and patience to help get me back on track better than the physical therapist! You taught me that I needed to strengthen the right muscles to relieve my injuries and to get stronger. I feel so much better and hope to be able to continue with your help. I hope to sign up for the third time to continue my program with your guidance.
—Jo Baudoin, event planner / small-business owner

As I approached my 60th birthday, I decided it was time to make some positive changes in my life. I was 25 pounds overweight and had very little muscle tone ... so I decided to sign up for four sessions with Matt, hoping I could find a way to finally make some progress. His targeted training and dietary advice made all the difference in helping me improve my overall health and pride in the way I look. I lost 25 pounds and have muscle tone I haven't had since I was 20 years old ... two years later

I continue to improve my physical health and emotional well-being without slipping back into bad habits. I highly recommend Matt to anyone who is serious about making a positive change in their health and physical appearance.

—Rob Tepper, geologist

My clients stay with me for the long run because of the relationships and bonds we build, as well as the results they enjoy. I'm proud to say I've changed their lives and have become an essential part of their continued success.

Anyway, if you want to join the team, please email me at SteppingUpInLife@gmail.com and write in the subject heading, "I'm Ready." I'll take it from there.

If you'd like more intensive one-on-one coaching from me, I have two specific programs that may interest you.

COACHING OPPORTUNITY #1: COMPETE AS AN ATHLETE IN THE GAME OF LIFE EXECUTIVE PROGRAM

If you're a high-powered executive grappling with back pain and joint pain, this will help you change the game, providing the following:

- Individual- or group-customized program of stretches and strengthening exercises to work on all areas of your body that exhibit muscular imbalances

- Ongoing coaching, nutritional guidance, and assessments to ensure you are following the program appropriately

- A nine-month commitment for those serious about alleviating their pain and improving their quality of life

This isn't a weight loss program, nor is it about cardio workouts or sports performance training. This is a program meant specifically to address the negatives of the executive lifestyle, to help you become more active, and to reduce your pain.

Please email me at **athleteinthegameoflife@ gmail.com** to get started. I will respond within twenty-four hours.

COACHING OPPORTUNITY #2: COMPETING AS AN ATHLETE IN THE GAME OF LIFE ACTIVE AGING PROGRAM

If you're sixty-five-plus and concerned about physical and mental decline, this program is designed to help you feel ageless, especially if you're …

- Someone dedicated to improving their quality of life

- Someone who may already be physically active and wants higher-quality results

- Someone ready to commit to a twelve-month plan to ensure safe progressions

Like the executive coaching program, this is *not* a weight loss program and it is not about cardio exercises or sports performance. This is to help you alleviate pain, become more mobile, and keep feeling younger and healthier. If you're interested, again, please email me at athleteinthegameoflife@gmail.com.

Finally, for more about me and to get more information about my programs, please visit my website at **mattpeale.com**. Thanks for giving this book a read, and I hope to work with you in the future, to keep you active and feeling good in all aspects of your life!

ABOUT THE AUTHOR

 att Peale has always loved playing sports and working out. He has played almost every sport on a recreational or competitive level since first grade and began doing pull-ups and push-ups in his room in eighth grade. Matt played soccer at Mandeville High School in Mandeville, Louisiana, before playing two years at the University of Southern Mississippi, where he earned his bachelor of science degree in marketing in 1997. After working in sales, Matt found his way into the fitness industry in 2008 as a personal trainer at 24 Hour Fitness in Laguna Hills, California. His journey led him back to Mississippi in

2011 and back to his high-school home in 2015. Over the years, Matt has spoken at healthy-lifestyle events, conducted professional-development seminars, and briefly hosted a talk show on a local New Orleans–area digital platform. As a loyal member of the Who Dat Nation, Matt never misses a Saints game, watching in person or on TV. He dreams of attending the World Cup one day and traveling to every continent. For more on Matt, please visit **mattpeale.com**.